Black's Picture Sports
TABLE TENNIS

Jill Hammersley-Parker has been ranked among the top ten table tennis players in the world. She has won the English national title a record seven times, became European singles and doubles champion in 1976, and has won numerous other open titles all over the world. Her personality and sportsmanship have become equally renowned and in 1979 she was awarded the MBE. She is married to the England table tennis captain, Donald Parker, with whom she created the Jill Hammersley-Parker Foundation for aiding promising young players.

Richard Eaton is racket sports correspondent of *The Sunday Times* and table tennis correspondent of *The Guardian*. He broadcasts on BBC radio, has contributed to newspapers and magazines all over the world, and is co-author of two other books on table tennis. He is an enthusiastic coach and player of several racket sports and is author of the book *Playing for Life* in The Sunday Times Activity series.

Black's Picture Sports

TABLE TENNIS

Jill Hammersley-Parker and
Richard Eaton

A & C Black · London

First published 1985 by A & C Black
(Publishers) Ltd
35 Bedford Row, London WC1R 4JH

Hammersley-Parker, Jill
Black's picture sports table tennis.
1. Table tennis
I. Title   II. Eaton, Richard
796.34'6   GV1005

ISBN 0-7136-5508-9

All photographs by kind permission of All-Sport
Photographic Limited.

Typeset by August Filmsetting, St. Helens.
Printed and bound in Great Britain by
J. W. Arrowsmith Ltd, Bristol.

Contents

Introduction

If you choose to play table tennis you may become part of the most popular pastime and sport of all. More people all around the world play the game in their homes than any other. More countries are affiliated to the International Table Tennis Federation than to the United Nations. More countries take part in the World Table Tennis Championships than in any other sporting event outside the Olympics.

Table tennis is cheap and easy. Those at school or at college or who are unemployed, or the young or the aged, or the small or the large, or even the physically handicapped, can play the game quite well. And on a higher level, the remarkable combination of speed and touch necessary to win makes it one of the most testing and thrilling international sports of all.

Table tennis began towards the end of the last century and the first bat is said to have been a cigar box lid! Later a bat shaped like a banjo made the noises which led to the game being called 'ping pong'. When it was discovered that this was the trade name of a well-known company, it was decided in 1927 to change the name of the game's first organisation to the Table Tennis Association.

Now more than half a century later, table tennis has a supporting organisation that aims to give every beginner the chance to start along the right lines. There are coaches in every region and county, and almost every sizeable town. If a coach is not attached to your local club then there will probably be several at other nearby clubs. The English Table Tennis Association (E.T.T.A.) or the International Table Tennis Federation (I.T.T.F.) are ready, willing and able to help you if you need to know where to go (for the Associations' telephone numbers and addresses see page 79).

Don't leave it too late—bad habits come quickly and disappear more slowly. Have a little coaching immediately. Mastering the basics is the hardest thing, but once you have done this try putting what you have learned to the test in matches. An extensive network of leagues ranges all over Britain, and it caters for a whole variety of attitudes and standards in the game. The lowest are modest indeed.

It is a good idea to play matches because not only will you have fun, you will also develop your skill at winning. The sport is full of players with ability who never learn to be effective. Have coaching but at the same time learn from the experience of matchplay.

If you develop the confidence and ability to compete and win matches, then consider tournament play. This may place greater demands upon you because you are pitched in on your own, but in turn you may derive more enjoyment and achieve much improvement. There are a tremendous number of different standard tournaments—club tournaments, town tournaments and county tournaments in England, and a comparable network in other countries too. Some are graded according to standard and prize money, such as one-star, two-star and three-star. This gives a good chance of competing against players at your own level.

Many of you may feel that you only want to play for fun. But you will get much more fun by at least being a little bit organised in what you do. If you go about table tennis aimlessly, you will get bored. Set yourself one or two aims—to master a stroke, or to play well enough to take part in a league, or at least to better your play.

Targets like these give you purpose. Targets only put you under pressure if they are unrealistic. So no matter how small or unimportant they may be to other people, take pride in them. At the same time, enjoy yourself as much as you can. It's only given to a very few to make it to the top.

Table tennis is very much a social game. Clubs are often attached to institutions like the local post office, or the gas company or the youth club. The E.T.T.A. has also been trying to encourage clubs in sports centres. If you prefer to play outside your home—and that is usually the way to have more fun and to learn—then join one of these clubs. A list can be obtained from the E.T.T.A.

You will almost certainly not be put off by what you find. Some sports clubs have an atmosphere that seems formidable or a little overwhelming to a beginner. Table tennis clubs normally don't. They are usually full of down-to-earth people playing a simple but delightful game. You should make friends quickly.

1 The Game

The game of table tennis is ridiculously easy. A net of 15·25 cm in height divides a table into two halves, each 1·37 m by 1·525 m. The ball must be returned into the opposite half by each opponent. Almost everybody finds this possible, which offers much encouragement to the beginner. Rather fewer can do it well and that offers an interesting challenge.

A white line marks the edges of the table and if the ball strikes these it is considered a fair shot, even if it shoots away at an unplayable angle. If the ball hits the side of the table it is considered off the table. Unique among the racket sports, in table tennis you do not volley the ball (i.e. hit it before it bounces), thus making the game much more simple.

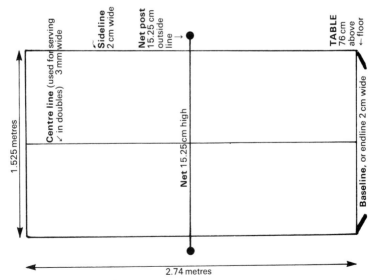

Fig. 1 The table and net.

There is only one other mark which you should find on the table. From the middle of the baseline to the middle of the net there can sometimes be a very thin line, marked in for doubles play. Partners in doubles must hit the ball alternately (i.e. in turn) and they must also serve in turn. They serve alternately from each side of their end of the table and the ball has to go diagonally into the opposite quarter on the other side of the net. The very thin white line marks out the quarter.

Scoring

Both in singles and in doubles the scoring ceases and a player, or doubles team, wins one game when he has 21 points, provided that he has a lead of at least two points. If he leads by one, the scoring goes on till a player does lead by two points (i.e. 21–19, 22–20, 23–21 etc.) Each player serves five consecutive points and then receives five times and continues doing this until the score reaches 20–20, in which case each player serves alternately once each.

One game, however, does not constitute a whole match in proper competitive play. The winner is the player who first has two games (in a match comprising the best of three games) or first has three games (in the best of five games). Best of three games is more common except in international play. The players change ends after each game, and also when one player reaches ten points in the final game.

Rules

Although the scoring and, indeed, the game itself are basically extremely simple, there are inevitably many rules. This is to enable officials to cope with all the possibilities that might occur. Most of these rules need not worry us at this stage—it is enough to know that you can obtain a copy of them either from your nearest club or from the E.T.T.A. We should perhaps just remember a few of the most important ones.

Many of the rules concern the service, which is delivered by making the ball bounce once on your own side of the table before bouncing on the other side. You must make sure, for instance, that your hand is flat when the ball is in it. Both bat and hand must be above the table. You must also toss the ball up straight and there must be no spin on it. Tossing the ball backwards is illegal, and so is stamping and serving with your back to the table. (For further details see Chapter 5 on service.) Since 1983, all players are obliged to have different colours on each side of the bat, a rule designed to help players tell which rubber is being used, if the opponent has decided to use a combination bat. There are a number of possible combinations of rubbers but it is far better to start with the same rubber on each side. Only after mastering the basics should you consider making use of the varieties of spin which can be achieved from a combination bat that requires more skill from its handler, as well as from the opponent.

Equipment

There are three different types of bat—*slow* for defensive play; *medium* for all-round play; *fast* for attacking play. There are many variations, depending on the wood, the sponge and the rubber. The wooden blade of the bat can be of one-, three-, five-, or seven-ply wood, but five-ply is the most usual. Soft wood will slow the ball up and make it good for defenders; hard wood helps to achieve a greater amount of spin or speed. If you use a hardwood you need to have very good ball control. It is probably better not to start with a blade that is too fast.

Sponge is usually attached to the rubber and comes in different thicknesses—1 mm, 1·5 mm, 2 mm or 2·5 mm. The total thickness of both sponge and rubber must not exceed 4 mm. Soft sponge can be married to a hard wood for a fast bat.

There are so many different types of rubber used on bats available on the market today that it is sometimes hard to keep up with all the varieties. Pimples on the rubber vary between 1 mm and 2·5 mm in length and they also vary in thickness. Probably the most common type of surface, however, is the one with pimples inwards: reversed rubber is usually called 'reverse' for short. The playing surface is smooth and gives the maximum amount of spin and speed. Provided it is not too fast it can be a good idea to start with this surface on both sides. (For further discussion on materials see Chapter 11.)

Clothing

You are not allowed to wear white in competitive table tennis because it would make it difficult for your opponent to see the ball. Clothing must be of one colour except for a one-centimetre trim. Some players play in striped, spotted or multi-coloured clothing, without it apparently affecting opponents' play and it would be nice to see this aspect of the game brought more up-to-date. It would help a lot of young players to play the game looking neat and smart instead of being dressed in scruffy jeans and tee-shirts. However, until this happens you will have to stick to plain shirts and shorts or skirts.

Ideal table tennis shoes should have good rubber soles that are not too thin. Socks need to have cushioning. If you play a lot, and certainly if you play in tournaments, you will cover a tremendous amount of ground. Some floors are hard and it is easy to get blisters. You should not have much difficulty finding the clothing you need. Fig. 2 of Jill Hammersley-Parker and Desmond Douglas shows you how you should look.

Fig. 2
The right clothing.

2 Grip and Stance

Grip

First you need to grip the bat properly. Hold it so that it feels comfortable, which may be slightly loosely—but not so loose that there is a danger of the bat falling out of your hand, nor too tight that you lose some feeling. On certain shots, it is very important to have plenty of feeling. Some players have what is known as a 'good hand', which means they have sensitivity of feeling and a good touch with the ball. This is a natural gift but it still needs to be built up. When you get nervous you may tend to hold the bat a bit tighter and that's when you lose feel and are most likely to make mistakes.

Western/Shakehands grip

Most good players in Europe have what is called a Western grip, also described as a shakehands grip. This describes what you should do with the bat very well. Most players also put their forefingers along the blade (see fig. 3 on p. 14) where the end of the finger goes pretty well to the edge. Some players curl that finger round the handle and Hasegawa, the famous Japanese player, even used to put his finger right in the middle of the blade! This is very unorthodox and it is almost certainly best to do what is shown in the photograph.

The other side of the shakehands grip is shown in fig. 4. The thumb just touches the rubber. Some players put their thumb up the blade for hitting backhands, as for instance does England's Nicky Jarvis. This is all right if it feels comfortable, but don't do it for a forehand shot or you might end up by hitting your thumb. The photograph also shows the butt of the

Fig. 3 The shakehands grip on reversed rubber.

Fig. 4 The shakehands grip on pimpled rubber.

14

hand well up so that there is an inch of handle showing. This is usually the best way to start.

Penholder grip
The only other grip you might use is the penholder. The Chinese players are famous for holding the bat with a penholder grip (see fig. 5), although in recent years they have been increasingly using the Western shakehands grip. With the penholder you hold the bat as though you are using chopsticks and the bat works like a pendulum. The trouble is that you can be limited because you use only one side of the bat and you have to cover more ground that way. One point in favour of the penholder grip is that it takes fractionally less time than the Western grip in turning round from the forehand to the backhand and back again. In fast rallies this can be important. However, this advantage is probably outweighed by the weakness on the penholder backhand which is sometimes a very awkward shot. (The backhand is played on the left side of the body for a righthander, and the forehand on the right side.)

Fig. 5 The penholder grip.

Stance

After a good grip, a good stance is important. Stand an arm's length away from the table with your weight on the insides of your feet, rather than on your toes. Your weight should be only slightly forwards, not too much. You may need to move backwards quickly as well as forwards or to either side. Being able to move quickly and being well prepared is vital at any standard of play. You may wish to have a slightly different stance depending on whether you play principally as an attacker and usually move forwards, or as a defender and usually move back. If you are to be an attacking player you may also wish to stand over to the backhand side to be able to get in an early attack on the forehand.

These things should be decided after you know what kind of player you are going to be, and whether you have weaknesses to cover up. They will also depend upon your particular aptitudes and personality. Meanwhile, to begin with, stand in the middle, head slightly forward, knees slightly bent and bat held at waist level in front of you.

These may seem small points but they will become more and more important as you go on. Table tennis played well is a fast game and you need to be mobile and mentally alert. The Chinese do a great deal of work in shadow play (going through the motions of the game) with youngsters before they even hit a ball. That suggests how important footwork is.

Start with shots played close to the table: the backhand with a square stance and the feet a shoulder's width apart (facing the line of play); the forehand with a side to square stance, more sideways than square to the table. The square stance is used because you need to recover quickly between each shot to be prepared for the next one.

Weight should be transferred from the back foot to the front foot as you hit the forehand. This cannot be done with the backhand (with the square stance) but you should still lean forwards as you hit the ball to give weight to the shot. Later, when you play shots away from the table, the stances and the footwork will vary.

Control is particularly important to build up. Many young players try to hit the ball too hard too soon. Better to get the feel of the ball and gradually build up your sense of touch using your arm and wrist.

Try to practise putting the ball to a good length, then short and low, both of which will make it harder for your opponent to attack. You should not put the ball too short, too long or too high. Play the ball backhand to backhand diagonally across the table first of all while you are learning these shots.

Later, when you have practised the same on the forehand, hit the ball down the line as well as diagonally across the table. The diagonal is the most common direction of attack even at quite a high level of play because it is easier, but it tends to make your shots predictable. Try to play the ball from backhand and forehand to three directions—diagonal, down the line, and to the middle. A shot to the middle can deny the opponent the room to make an attacking shot, or an effective angle from which to project it.

3 Spin

Table tennis is, above all, a game of spin. The vast majority of shots have some spin on them. The most basic tactic at all levels of the game is to fool your opponent about what kind of spin you are using, or to use the same kind of spin but in different amounts. This will cause the opponent to make mistakes.

Spectators often don't realise just how much spin a piece of thin bat rubber on a light celluloid ball can create. In recent years the technology of making bat rubbers has become so advanced that leading players have been enabled to do extraordinary things with the ball. Place your bat flat in the way of a shot from one of these players and the ball will often leap sideways off the table!

Beginners also frequently put some spin on the ball when they hit it, but they may not entirely be aware of it. Developing that awareness is essential. As soon as you do so, the game becomes alive with dazzling possibilities. There are three main types of spin: backspin, topspin and sidespin. The diagrams (figs. 6a, 6b and 6c) should make them clear.

Fig. 6a shows backspin. This occurs when the blade of the bat goes down underneath the ball and makes the ball go round, or rotate, anti-clockwise, i.e. back towards the striker. The bat will need to be tilted backwards to create this effect (called opening the bat).

Fig. 6b shows topspin. This occurs when the blade of the bat goes up and over the top of the ball and makes it rotate clockwise. The bat will usually be tilted slightly forwards to do this (called closing the bat). It can either be done with a brushing action over the top of the ball or with a more violent action of the arm and bat from near the floor to near the head.

Fig. 6c shows sidespin. This occurs when the bat comes round from behind the ball and round the side of it furthest away from

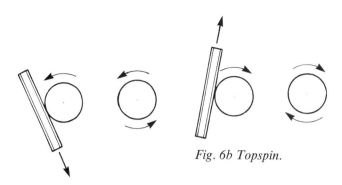

Fig. 6b Topspin.

Fig. 6a Backspin.

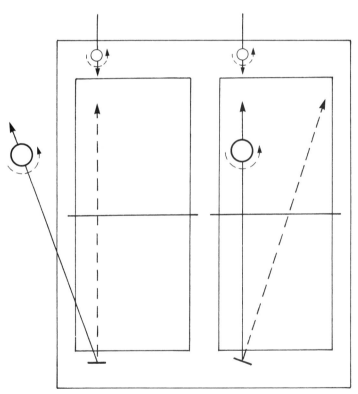

Fig. 6c Sidespin. This shows the effect of sidespin when the ball hits the bat and also how the bat should be angled to counteract sidespin.

19

the body. This is mostly done on the forehand and causes the ball to rotate sideways in an anti-clockwise direction. Backhand sidespin is sometimes used on service, when the bat is taken from left to right round the side of the ball nearest the body. The ball again spins in an anti-clockwise direction. Sidespin is usually the most difficult of the three and probably is best not attempted at an early stage unless it comes naturally. Backspin and topspin should be learned first.

Backspin is usually associated with defence and topspin with attack. Backspin shots normally pass low over the net, and topspin high over the net. Backspin makes the ball keep low when it bounces and slows it down. Topspin makes it bounce upwards and forwards and gather speed.

If you are facing a backspin shot you will find the ball tends to jump downwards from your bat into the net and you will need to lift it a little higher than usual. If you are facing topspin the ball will tend to jump upwards from your bat, high over the net and either off the end of the table or into such a weak position that the opponent's follow-up finishes the rally. You will need, therefore, to keep the ball down.

Creating backspin and topspin can be done solely with the arm. You will have a more open bat for backspin and a more closed one for topspin, and will create greater or lesser spin by simply altering the angle of your bat. Indeed, after a little while a great deal of deception can be created by doing this, keeping the opponent guessing how much or how little spin is on the ball.

Spin is very much associated, however, with the action of the wrist. It is wrist that gives variety and deception and also some of the game's most brilliant shots. You need complete control of the bat and ball before you attempt this, but several things will help—time to produce the shot (don't attempt it when you are under pressure), correct grasp of the bat (hold a little more tightly) and, naturally enough, a strong wrist. It is often easier to put spin on the ball if the second bounce is coming to you off the end of the table. You can then take your bat below the height of the table and, whether you are backspinning the ball or topspinning it, you will then be able to put so much more into the shot.

4 Push and Drive

Sweden, which has produced such a great number of outstanding players in recent years, has interesting theories about teaching youngsters. They are first taught how to attack rather than to push, which is often the custom elsewhere. The advantage of this method is that if a player is under pressure in a match, he or she tends instinctively to go back to what was first learned. In the past it meant that Swedish players were more likely to feel comfortable attacking in a crisis and were unlikely to become overly tentative and anxious.

This policy, however, is probably best suited to more able players. There are many ambitious young players who have become captivated by the idea of making flashy topspins and spectacular-looking loop attacking shots too soon. They often do so before developing proper ball control or eliminating basic weaknesses. In any case, defensive skills are a very much underestimated part of table tennis.

It is usually safest to start by learning the push and drive. Learn them in a special order—backhand push and forehand drive, then backhand drive and forehand push. The forehand push is usually the most difficult.

While learning these shots try to make contact with the ball at the top of its bounce. By making contact at the same height each time it helps you develop timing. If you learn to take the ball either earlier or later, then it may become your natural instinct to do that. It is easier to teach someone who takes the ball earlier to be an attacker and someone who takes it later to be a defender. Whichever you eventually become depends partly on your personality as well as your abilities.

When you start there can be a tendency just to push the ball anywhere on the table. Don't let this happen. Used with purpose the push helps build up ball control and confidence.

Backhand Push

To play the backhand push (with which you will be able to cover more of the table than the forehand) put your right leg in and play the shot with your legs about a shoulder's width apart. As you get better at it you may not need to move your body round so much and you will play more square on to the table. Even so, your right leg should be in front. At first it may be better to play the push, go back to the ready position, then play the shot again, so as to get used to the footwork and movement required.

The bat moves about three to four feet, about the length of an arm. The upper part of the arm does not move much; the forearm does most of the work. It goes through until the arm almost straightens. The weight is transferred from the left leg to the right. The body does not turn much. The head is down a little. Make sure you watch the ball very carefully.

You can see most of these things in the sequence of photographs (figs. 7a–7d). The first picture shows the weight slightly forwards with the bat just above waist height. The second shows the bat moving forwards and it is already starting to tilt back a little bit; the weight is going further forwards. In the third picture the weight is even further forward and the bat

Fig. 7a The backhand push.

Fig. 7b

is tilted back still more, just after the ball has been struck. The bat has travelled two feet over the table and the right foot has almost gone under the table. The fourth picture shows the extent to which the bat goes under the ball on the backhand push. Although the weight goes forwards quite significantly, it is not so much that it prevents quick recovery to the ready position.

You can put spin on the push with a 'dig' at the ball as you make contact. It is not necessary to use much wrist action, although some players do. Attacking players are less likely to use wrist action because they may want to touch the ball just over the net, very short, denying the opponent room to attack. Then they will try to get in first to attack. But a push with backspin, as in the series of photographs, is not a soft stroke. When building up control you may start by playing the ball softly, but if you want to put spin on you must really dig the ball. The bat moves quite quickly through the air. It is important, as you get better, to vary the spin—if you want more spin use more action of the wrist. The varied angle of the bat can give more or less spin too.

Sometimes a defender will place pushes at different heights to entice the opponent to hit. Although it can be a good tactic, it should not perhaps be attempted against a good attacking

. 7c

Fig. 7d

player. If an opponent only hits occasionally, different heights can be used as a temptation. There will be the risk of a winner but on many occasions the hit may miss. Pushing the ball high down the middle of the table denies the opponent an angle to strike a winner. On the other hand it is best to push towards an opponent's weakness. A clever opponent may aim the ball towards your right hip which is one of the most awkward shots to receive for a righthander.

Forehand Drive

On the forehand drive turn side to square and take the bat back further than you would for the backhand hit. Don't take it right back behind your body at this stage, though, but just in line with your body. Then swing forwards again, hitting through the ball and transferring your weight from the right to the left leg. Make sure as you hit the ball that your arm is roughly at right angles to your body—not in too close and not out too far. The bat should finish above the ball again, with your arm almost straight. With the forehand, the more powerful stroke, it is important to put a bit of topspin on the ball to make sure it goes over the net and onto the table. You can apply spin quite naturally with the forehand hit by slightly turning the bat over the ball on impact and continuing it on the follow-through.

The forehand drive is not a shot that you play solely with the movement of your arm: you should follow through across your body. It is also necessary to make sure that your body goes into the shot as you transfer your weight from your right foot to the left. Some coaches say that the bat should finish above the head but it is usually the most natural thing to swing it across your body and not up. This helps you to drive 'through' the ball and eventually aids the development of a more penetrating forehand 'kill' or 'smash'.

The drive especially will stand the defender in very good stead, particularly when coming back to the table to finish off a rally from a 'drop shot' or a push that has been put up too high. And the 'roll' made with a little wrist action, which is a natural development of the hit, will provide a good basis for players going on to develop loop and topspin shots (as discussed in Chapters 7 and 8).

Backhand Drive

The photographs on page 26 (figs. 8a and 8b) show a backhand drive being played from a fairly comfortable position close to the table. It is struck across the table to the opposite corner. This is how you should try to practise and learn the shot.

Unlike the forehand drive, the body is almost square to the table and the bat, as in the first picture, is taken back to the waist. The left leg is slightly behind the right and the weight goes forwards on to the front foot, as in the second picture. It is a quick stroke, with much less backswing and the ball is struck flat. The follow through finishes above the point of impact and the wrist should naturally turn over slightly but there is little or no topspin. The arm almost straightens to its full length and the bat finishes at about shoulder height. But be prepared for a quick recovery to the ready position.

It is worth emphasising just how important it is to watch the ball closely. You can see this very well from the first picture which was taken immediately before the impact of ball and bat. The head is coming slightly down here. Compare this with the second picture where the head has come up again and the eyes are still on the ball. That downward and upward movement of the head obviously has to be made fairly late in the ball's flight, and it is often a good idea to check to see whether you are doing this consistently.

For most people the forehand side may be the more natural side for hitting and the backhand the natural side for pushing. There is, however, more scope for a longer push on the forehand, provided that you get side to square.

Forehand Push

The forehand push needs the left leg forward, but otherwise many of the basics are similar to the backhand. The bat may tilt less and come through at less of an open angle. This means you are likely to hit more of the back of the ball on the forehand push, and more of the bottom of the ball on the backhand push.

The backhand push can often be played from nearly straight in front of you, almost square on to the table, but a longer and

Fig. 8a The backhand drive.

Fig. 8b

26

sometimes more effective stroke can be made on the forehand if you get round sideways. This helps give you more spin if you do it properly, but you may need to be quick at moving your body.

Having learned to turn sideways you can often learn to play the push off the 'wrong' foot on both forehand and backhand shots (this would be right foot for forehand, left foot for backhand). It can be a useful way of shaping for the shot if the ball is short. You may have to lean close to the table to do it and you won't have quite the same length of stroke because you will be square on. It may be a very simple, basic stroke but it can often be very effective even at high level.

An example of the forehand push is shown in the photograph below which was taken at the 1977 World Championships in Birmingham. The push is being played square on, off the 'wrong' foot, i.e. the right foot. It probably occurred after a spell of defending away from the table when the opponent made a sudden 'drop shot' or short push. On these occasions the aim is to push the ball back short and low.

Fig. 9 The forehand push.

This short touch over the net has become an important stroke in modern table tennis, especially on return of serve against an attacker. If the ball is controlled well there is little that can be done with it. It is too difficult to open up the attack on that sort of ball and the only reply is to trade push for push. Then each player tries to induce the other to put the ball up a fraction higher or longer and so make way for an attacking shot.

5 The Service

The serve has become very important in recent years. At one time the main object was just to put the ball into play. Now it is very different: if you can win ten points on your serve in a game, which is perfectly feasible, it can win you a match. The great advance in the variety of bat rubbers and spin has helped make this possible. Even if your serve does not win the point, the return of serve can be made to come back too high. Then there is every chance of making a good follow-up, sometimes called third ball attack. There are several different ways of serving well and here are some of the basic ones.

Sidespin Serve

The sidespin service on the backhand is a good one to use regularly. The ball must be placed flat in the palm and tossed upwards without applying spin from the hand as this is against the rules.

With the sidespin serve you need to make sure it goes either short or very long—but not half-length because this is easy to attack. If it is short it should be safe from attack but serves near the baseline can also be difficult for the opponent, particularly if you vary the direction.

As you see in fig. 10a the ball is tossed a few inches and the wrist dropped so that the bat moves towards the body, inside the ball. It is possible to draw the bat right across the body as in fig. 10b. The more you do this and the faster, the more spin will be put on the ball. When it bounces it will move out towards the opponent's forehand. It will be particularly difficult to take if aimed at the body.

Fig. 10a Backhand sidespin   *Fig. 10b*
  serve.

The direction of the serve should, of course, vary, just as the length should. Do not allow an opponent to get used to a particular kind of serve. The sort you deliver will depend on the opponent's strong or weak points. Serve short more often to a player who attacks and full length more often to an opponent who does not.

Backspin Serve

The sidespin serve can be varied with an ordinary backspin serve, in which the bat goes underneath the ball in a similar motion to the backhand push. The bat will then follow through straight forward, away from the body instead of across it, which makes a big difference. The preparation for this serve should be very similar to the sidespin serve, so that the opponent cannot tell which serve it is until after the ball has been struck. Often the serves will be mixtures of sidespin and backspin.

It is usually easier to do a sidespin serve on the backhand side because the arm can move freely across the body and it is therefore a natural action. With the forehand sidespin serve the body is in the way and the resulting action can appear and feel a little cramped—see the sequence of pictures, figs. 11a–11c. But it can still be very effective. Carole Moore who gets a lot of leverage with her wrist, executes the sidespin very well.

In fig. 11a of this sequence the stance is half sideways and the eyes are on the ball. This time there is room for the bat to be taken back further, even though there is less room for the follow-through. The wrist is fairly loose and also slightly bent back.

On impact the bat is almost vertical and the spin comes mostly from the wrist. Although you do get some spin from the arm as well, the action of the arm is limited. You can see this most clearly in fig. 11c where the follow-through comes as far as

Fig. 11a Forehand sidespin serve.

the left-hand side of the body but no further. The serve has been delivered from about two feet from the table. It is generally not a good idea to vary this since it aids control of length of the serve, but it is advisable to vary which part of the table you serve from. You can, in fact, serve from any part to any you wish. Make sure your service action has a quick recovery into the ready position.

Forehand Sidespin and Chop Serve

The forehand sidespin and chop serve from a crouch position (see figs. 12a and 12b on pages 32 and 33) can be a useful variation from the usual serves. Bettine Vriesekoop, of

Fig. 11b   *Fig. 11c*

Fig. 12a Forehand sidespin chop serve. Note the bat handle down and the head up.

Holland, the 1982 European champion, often uses it. The stance has to be low because you are hitting down, and the point of contact is low. If you were to hit the ball from a higher point it would produce too bouncy a delivery.

A great advantage of this delivery is that you can serve round the side of the ball to give it sidespin, or under the bottom of the ball to give it backspin, both with a similar action. The photographs show the ball being served from the forehand corner but it can be served from anywhere with a quick recovery. You will get more spin from this serve if you deliver it long, because then you can put more effort into it and can let the

Fig. 12b

wrist really go—the wrist can go further in a forward direction than when it is moving sideways to keep the ball short.

A problem with this serve is that it is difficult to throw the ball up straight, as the rules demand. It is a matter of interpretation as to how straight you must throw it but many players do in fact propel it rather a long way back and could, in theory, be penalised. You are not supposed to obtain spin by doing this; as you can see from photograph *b* the ball is not spinning. You would only get a great deal of spin by tossing the ball up high in the air.

Players who first achieved spin quite legally, and to great effect, were Chinese. They often throw the ball up to tremendous heights, fifteen feet or more, to obtain spin (see the next photograph of Guo Yue-hua, the 1981 and 1983 world

Fig. 13 Guo Yue-hua playing a high toss serve.

champion). The Chinese are renowned for winning points outright from their serves, and the higher the ball is thrown the more spin can be obtained. This is because the ball is travelling fast as it hits the bat.

You can put different spins on the high toss serve by sticking the bat in at different angles at the last moment. Players with supple wrists do this very quickly and it is not easy to detect. This kind of serve first attracted a lot of attention during the world championships in Birmingham in 1977, although the

Chinese were doing it long before then. It is not easy because it makes great demands on timing; however, European players are now perfecting the technique even though it is easier to tell from the wrist action of a Western grip player what sort of spin is being put on the ball.

A few words of warning. Remember that since 1983–4 the rules about serving have changed a great deal. Now you must not place the bat or the ball below the table before serving as players used to do to hide which side of the bat they were about to use. Nor must you stamp your foot which some players once did to hide the noise of different bat rubbers on the ball. Also, you must not stand with your back to the table and serve round your body, or from behind the body. There are, however, equally effective and far simpler methods of keeping your opponent guessing.

Return of Serve

With the increased importance of service, return of serve has become crucial too. We have already stressed the importance of the ready position. For the return of serve you should stand slightly nearer to the table if you have a 'close-to-the-table' style like Desmond Douglas. As you can see from the photograph of Desmond, Jill Hammersley-Parker and Jimmy Walker about an arm's length from the table is usually about right. Your legs

Fig. 14 Stance for return of serve.

should be slightly apart and your knees bent, to be ready for a quick, early movement.

Desmond is standing over to the left because he will be trying to attack straight away with his lefthanded forehand. Jimmy, a fellow former England international, is righthanded, and so stands over the other side to do the same with his forehand. A defensive player will stand in the middle because this kind of player must be ready to move to either side. Attacking players may be more balanced with their weight forwards, ready to move in, whereas the placing of a defensive player's weight must facilitate movement in any direction.

Receiving service may not always be easy. Your opponent has the initiative and, if used properly, a serve can force the receiver into difficulties. If your opponent is putting you under pressure on serve your aim will be to contain it, probably with a push, keeping it low and short or in a safe position. If your opponent is serving to put the ball in a safe place, then try to take the initiative yourself.

It was clear from fig. 14 that there are different stances. Desmond's and Jimmy's (both over to the backhand—one for a lefthander, the other a righthander) are adopted with attack in mind. Although it is best to develop an all-round game to deal with whatever your opponent dishes up, you still need to take up a ready position in relation to a specific line of play.

Make sure you watch the server closely, and as the server starts to move, so should you. It takes an important fraction of a second to get moving, and if you wait until the ball has been hit you may be too slow. Your feet should be moving slightly in the ready position, without losing your balance. Watch closely the opponent's wrist and elbow to spot deceptions. Then watch the flight and bounce of the ball carefully to detect the spin.

The server will be trying to deceive you, so you should try to do the same. Vary the return. If you are trying to contain the serve (or to play safe), play it short to different parts of the table. Or, if it goes long, return it so it is wide and difficult to reach, perhaps wide to the forehand. If you successfully contain the server and prevent an attack on the third ball, *you* could try to attack.

6 Defence—Chop and Float

The defender's basic shot is the chop which, like the push, imparts backspin to the ball. The chop, however, is a much longer shot and very often creates a great deal more spin. The ball may rotate backwards so much that the attacker cannot stop the ball being dragged downwards as it touches his bat. This may take it into the net or force him to lift the ball. Then he may send it off the end of the table or set up a high ball for an easy kill.

The chop is obviously more effective if it is used with a variety of spin, sometimes heavy, sometimes light. It is better still if the opponent can be deceived into thinking there is spin on the ball when actually there is none at all. This is done with the float, a shot which appears similar to the chop but instead has little or no backspin. Opponents may make more mistakes against a float than against a chop because of its better disguise.

Backhand Chop

With the backhand chop the bat is taken back almost to shoulder height and then is brought down, slicing behind and underneath the ball. Contact is made below the waist and just in front of the player. This is shown in figs. 15a–15c on pages 38 and 39. In the first picture the weight is more on the back foot. In the second, just before the moment of impact, the weight is evenly distributed. In the third the weight is transferred to the front foot. The follow-through continues until the arm straightens. It is a longer stroke than people sometimes imagine.

The position of the body is practically sideways to the table, and this is necessary on the backhand to have free movement of

Fig. 15a The backhand chop.

the bat. It is possible to get away with being more square on with the forehand chop, perhaps turning from the waist or altering the angle of the wrist instead. It is better though to be side-to-square, even if under pressure this will not always be possible.

A heavier chop requires more wrist and a quicker action. Conversely, there will be less spin from a less vigorous action. This is one of the reasons why it is usually possible to detect a heavily chopped ball. A chop with a medium amount of wrist and mixed with a float shot can be hard to detect.

Before using wrist a beginner needs to perfect the basic stroke first. Learn to control the ball well. If there is too much wrist to start with, control may be more difficult. At first the chop should be played mainly from the arm. Once the ball can be returned regularly in this way, then wrist can be added. The more the bat is opened, the more spin will be created.

Fig. 15b   Fig. 15c

The Float

The principal difference in the appearance of the chop and the float shots is the angle of the bat. The float, apparently played in a similar fashion, in fact has the bat in a more upright position. There is some slight spin imparted to the ball, but the bat strikes much more through the back of the ball than underneath it.

This difference in the bat angle can be difficult to see from the other end of the table, and possibly may even be hidden from the opponent. But from the side it becomes obvious that there is a difference in the way the bat is tilted, as you can see from figs. 16a–16c on pages 40 and 41. Compare the first in the sequence, fig. 16a, with the first in the sequence for the backhand chop, fig. 15a. The angle of the bat at this stage (and the whole preparation) does not look very different.

Compare the second set of photographs, figs. 15b and 16b. With the backhand chop the bat has turned under the ball to a more horizontal angle, while with the backhand float the bat is nearly vertical, or upright. In the third comparable photographs, figs. 15c and 16c, these points are emphasised even

Fig. 16a The backhand float.

more. The weight has come forwards on the right foot in much the same way and the positions of the head and body are much the same, but the angles of the bat are very different.

If the follow-through has been made close to the end of the table, the opponent may not be able to tell what has happened. However, for the float the upright bat position has stayed almost the same throughout the shot, whereas for the chop the bat has turned underneath the ball.

As mentioned earlier, the float, because of its disguise, is more likely to bring a mistake from an opponent. It is, therefore, a useful ploy to float the ball back if you are forced further away from the table or too wide (i.e. to the side of the table). It may help you recover from a difficult situation.

Forehand Chop

The forehand chop is played, if possible, from a side to square position. The bat comes up to shoulder height in the prepar-

Fig. 16c

ation but because the playing arm is this time behind the body the backswing can be longer. The weight goes back on the right foot and then is transferred to the left. Contact is made at about waist height—perhaps a little higher than the backhand—and the follow-through is only a short way in front of the body.

As said before, many players don't get into the right position for every stroke, except perhaps some of the Chinese or the top North Koreans who move extremely quickly. If you don't quite get into position you must compensate with the wrist, with a different bat angle, and different weight transference, all of which makes the shot more tricky.

Comparison of forehand chop and forehand float
Below are two sequences of four pictures comparing the forehand chop with the forehand float. The chop is in figs. 17a–17d, and the float in figs. 18a–18d (see over). Once again, in the first two pictures (figs. 17a and 18a) the bat angles are very similar. A shot is being played about four to five feet from the

41

Fig. 17a The forehand chop sequence.

Fig. 17b

Fig. 18a The forehand float sequence.

Fig. 18b

Fig. 17c

Fig. 17d

Fig. 18c

Fig. 18d

table, which is quite close for defending. This would probably be the third shot in the rally, i.e. before it has become necessary to settle into a more defensive position further back.

The second pair of pictures (figs. 17b and 18b) show that with the chop, the bat is turning under the ball just before impact, but is still upright with the float. The transference of weight is similar as it is in the third pair of pictures (figs. 17c and 18c). By this time the bat has become close to the horizontal on the chop, but it is still fairly upright on the float. In each case the bat has been making a complete downward movement as well as a forward movement.

Comparing the last two pictures in each sequence (figs. 17d and 18d), you can see that in each case the bat has made mostly a forward movement. But with the float the bat has finished further forwards. This is clearly seen from the side, but from the other end of the table it is probably not detectable. The feeling of a float is one of guiding the ball over, instead of sliding underneath it. The opponent may be surprised by the unsuspected lack of backspin.

Basic differences between a chop and a float
There are, however, other ways to pick out the differences between a chop and a float. Against a good defender you may need to use all of them to survive. You can sometimes tell by the flight of the ball, and possibly by the sound of the ball on the rubber. It may hang in the air more with a chop but curve higher in the air with a float.

Ideally, the defender plays the float back low over the net, but this is not always possible because the shot is one of the most difficult. If there is a lot of heavy topspin coming from the attacker, the float has to be 'cushioned over' so that the ball does not fly out of control. But this also makes it possible for the attacker to spot what is happening. By watching the ball very carefully in its flight, it is possible to see whether it is spinning round. If it is floated and there is no spin, some players can sometimes see the brand mark on it!

Here are two more photographs showing defensive chops. Fig. 19a shows a very determined forehand chop near the floor from a great distance back, probably twenty feet. If you are going to defend, you must be prepared for this to happen from time to time. A good attacking player will not play at the same pace all the time. Agility, flexibility and an ability to improvise

44

Fig. 19a Defensive forehand chop.

Fig. 19b

have, in this case, facilitated a well-balanced shot, even though there is a great deal of pressure and the weight is heavily down on the right foot. There has not been time to use the recommended positioning and footwork. But all may be well, provided as always there is a readiness to recover quickly. There may even be a drop shot, i.e. dropping the ball just over the net.

Fig. 19b shows a forehand chop, or float, closer to the table. The action picture gives a better idea than the posed one of the concentration and determination needed to defend successfully. Look how closely the eye is on the ball. This is essential when dozens of different spins are put on the ball, and the success or failure of your reply can often be measured in millimetres.

Qualities for Good Defence

It is valuable for a defender to have a naturally good eye, though co-ordination can be improved a certain amount through practice. There is also a need to gauge different distances quickly. A sense of timing is important, and this too can be improved through practice. Sometimes taking the ball early, or rushing it, can be the problem. You may be standing up too straight instead of bending your knees and getting down to the ball. You might have to slow down a little, let the speed come out of the ball (this happens more the longer it travels), and give yourself a chance to acquire a feeling of rhythm. This may be especially necessary if you are nervous. If you are too late on the shot you must make a conscious effort to prepare as early as possible next time. Try to work out what is happening. Sometimes the bat angle may be wrong. Good players often do these things instinctively.

Concentration, determination and quick movement have already been mentioned as important qualities for a defender. Each of these will be improved by fitness. There must also be a desire to keep the ball in play as well as a positive attitude to the game. The ability to control the rally with spins and the ability to chop and float with accuracy should be built up with regular practice.

A defender must also keep the ball low most of the time; too high and there could be trouble. If possible keep the ball near the baseline. It is usually more difficult for the attacking player to apply pressure when the ball is deep. If the ball lands half-table, it is easier to topspin; if it is high it is easier to smash. If you put the ball deep you can sometimes risk placing it a little higher to tempt the opponent. Variety is important: if you put the ball back with the same spin all the time your opponent will get used to it and will wait for the one that can be put away. Sometimes you should put heavy, medium, little, or no spin at all on it. Then the opponent will make more mistakes.

Beware, however, of the drop shot, as it can be used to break up a chop and float game. The attacker can even win the point outright with it. This is done by stopping the ball (against the lob, see Chapter 9) or lifting the ball (against the chop) so short that it bounces at least twice on the table. The defender, running in, may not reach it in time because he cannot let it drop below the height of the table. Even if he does reach it, to be moved in and out, as well as from side to side, can be very destructive to a defender's play.

The drop shot can only really be played effectively if the ball has been returned fairly short. Disguise and taking the ball early are the secrets of the shot's success. The ball is taken just after the bounce. To do that, it is vital to read correctly the spin on the ball and to get the bat angle right. The grip needs to be fairly relaxed to give feel, and the bat opened to lift a chop gently over the net. There is very little forward movement of the bat to prevent the ball going too far. If the shot is used against the lob or any topspin shot, then the bat comes over the ball at a closed angle and the ball is propelled downwards. But whichever kind of drop shot is used, the element of surprise is what makes it effective.

7 Attack

Driving and Topspinning

Driving and topspinning are important shots for beginners, as well as for more advanced players. It is essential for beginners to master the controlled drives before moving on to the more powerful topspin strokes. Many players have become so good that they are able to stand close to the table and play an aggressive drive against attacking shots from opponents. A fine example is England's Desmond Douglas. His counter-hitting ability is renowned.

Driving or hitting can be valuable for a defender too. It can be a sudden method of surprising the opponent if the attack has been withdrawn in favour of a push or a drop shot. The attacker may have misread the spin and popped the ball up a little. Then it can be a very satisfying moment for the defender to move close to the table and put the ball away! This can be done off either the forehand or the backhand.

Backhand Drive

Fig. 20 illustrates how this shot is particularly useful. If you are moving quickly towards the table, it is going to be far more convenient to be able to play the hit facing straight down the table. The backhand drive, remember, is comfortably played in a square on position, whereas the forehand drive requires you to get a little sideways to the table. In addition, you can cover most of the table with a backhand drive as you can play it directly in front of the body and you do not have to move the body out of the way. In the photograph the backhand drive has

Fig. 20 Disguised backhand drive.

been played from near the forehand corner of the table. The action of the body and the position of the bat over the table hint at what may have happened—the opponent has tried a short drop shot and a defensive situation has been transformed into a potentially attacking one. The backhand drive has been played crosscourt (i.e. across the table), but it might well have looked to the opponent as though it were about to be struck down the line. This sort of disguise is valuable; if you can achieve it the results are often dramatic.

However, it is not always wise to play a backhand drive from far across on the forehand side, as shown here. It depends on where you have been defending. If you have been chopping away from the middle of the table, then it would not be too difficult to move across to that side. But don't try to be too ambitious. You have to be well balanced to come in from a distance and play the ball accurately. You need to get into a moderately comfortable position—you can't just hit on the run.

The shot in fig. 20 has been hit reasonably well and is not too dissimilar from how it was described in Chapter 4. The bat has been taken straight back a short distance to the waist—this is a very quick stroke indeed. The wrist and the bat have been turned over the ball, but although the shot may have a little topspin it has really been hit fairly flat.

Apart from the disguise of direction, a further element of surprise will help. When the opponent sees the drop shot the expected reply is often a push. With no warning you can produce the hit, but remember it is sometimes not easy to do. It is all right if you are already near to the table but it is difficult if you are just coming in. You can come in too fast and probably overhit, you can get too far over the table, and sometimes you may not get there at all. Move quickly but remain well-balanced. It is best to develop the driving strokes in practice by standing in one position and grooving the shot. When the arm movements have become rhythmical, you can start to turn the body a little with the shot. Then finally add transference of weight from back foot to front, into the ready position, and back again quickly for the next hit.

It is vital to concentrate on driving the ball the same way each time. If you hit it in different ways you have more options but you are more likely to make important mistakes, especially while your game is still developing. Until you have a basic grooved drive it is wise to avoid variations in the path of the ball and in the angle of the bat. No matter how good your touch you need to build up your timing.

The Topspin Drive

When drives are developed into more powerful strokes they are often called topspin drives. Most of the power comes from the body and the forehand is the more powerful swing because the sideways stance enables extra weight to go into the shot. As we have already said, the backhand is played square on, and the power has to be generated mainly from the elbow and the wrist. The body and shoulder come into use far more with the forehand, and many players who use this shot may well content themselves with a block on the backhand, particularly if they play close to the table.

If you have developed a good drive in the early stages of learning the game (see Chapter 4), it will stand you in good stead for the topspin drive (discussed in the following chapter).

In some ways this is like a rolled drive except that it has a good deal more speed and spin.

Forehand Topspin Drive
Some players don't have backhand topspins and the forehand is the more common drive. Get into a side to square stance, with your left leg forward and start with the bat angled forward at about 45 degrees. Then there is an upward and forward movement from about two feet behind the body. It looks a fairly horizontal shot but the bat actually travels up and finishes by the head. At one time it used to be taught that topspin came from the elbow, but nowadays the emphasis is much more on the whole of the arm. At first you can just lift the ball up using your shoulder and elbow. As you get better use your wrist as well.

This shot is a very important and developing part of the modern game and a few players even learn to hit topspins from right over the table. This can alter the whole tactics of table tennis because it can cut out the push. When the topspin is done in this way the bat angle becomes even more closed and horizontal.

You can also play a topspin drive from a deep position, in other words from a long way back from the table. Some players can be particularly dangerous when they get away from the table—a position from which many players defend—and attack with the topspin drive. Dragutin Surbek of Yugoslavia, a former European champion, and Ann-Christin Hellman, Sweden's former number one, are good examples of players who have done this to great effect. You need to search to find the style that suits you best.

8 The Loop

It is generally easier to slow things down than to quicken them up, and very often people play faster than they need to. This partly explains the popularity of the loop, an attacking topspin shot that does what the name suggests, i.e. it loops with exaggerated spin on to the table. People also get rather carried away with the loop because it is so spectacular; it is more important to have an all-round game. The loop is, nevertheless, an important stroke and one that changed the game in favour of attackers when it was developed in the 'sixties.

After you have learned a hit and a roll it is a natural progression to go on to a topspin drive or loop. A loop shot also puts topspin on the ball. The main difference is that the shot is generally made in more of an upward direction, imparting a slower trajectory to the ball—the trajectory (i.e. the path of the ball in flight) of a loop. Its advantage is that great spin can be applied, making the ball kick and lurch forwards on impact with the table and frequently forcing the opponent back. It can also turn a position of no advantage into one of great advantage against a perfectly low, good length shot. Whoever gets in first with the loop often wins a rally. Its main disadvantage is that you need a ball whose second bounce will come off the end of the table—to give the room for the low preparation of the bat near the floor.

A few top players can loop over the top of the table but then the shot moves in a more horizontal direction, like a discus throw, and becomes similar to the power topspin drive. The 'feeling' of the loop is not easy to communicate; it is a sort of brushing motion, brushing the back of the ball. You make contact only lightly: the more lightly you do so the more spin you get. It is a difficult shot for the learner. You need the rubber to grip the ball well so you should not use an old piece of material.

Sometimes the stroke is taught by propping the net up so that a ball can run along the table from one end to the other. When it reaches the end the player tries to lift the ball over the net without hitting it into the end of the table. It is difficult. Most people cannot do the exercise because they don't bend their legs properly or get sufficiently low down to lift the ball up and over.

Forehand Loop

On the forehand loop you achieve drive from the legs. Look at figs. 21a–21d on pages 54 and 55. The legs are being bent and straightened, and the weight is transferred from the right leg, into the shot, and onto the left leg. There is a great deal of use of legs, arms, body and wrist. The more wrist you use, the more spin you are likely to get.

In the first photograph the bat has dropped down nearly to knee level as the ball approaches. In the second photograph the arm is straighter and the body bent lower. The wrist is bent back too. The third photograph in the sequence shows the arm at the point of contact, roughly at waist height. It is hard to say from this picture whether it is a dropping ball. It is best to take it at the peak of the bounce. Against a blocked ball you need to drive the ball harder, so your bat will travel more horizontally. Against a chopped ball it is necessary to give the ball more lift to counteract the backspin.

In the fourth picture the bat has ended up past the head. The spin has come from both the waist and the arm, as well as from the body and the legs, which have straightened. The bat should turn over on the follow through, and you recover quickly to the ready position.

Timing for the loop is very important because you are showing only a small amount of the bat face to the ball. The whole action is fairly quick and violent and this increases the need for control of the bat. It is easy to miss the ball altogether. It is a good idea to start with a slow loop and progress to a fast one.

Fig. 21a The forehand loop sequence.   *Fig. 21b*

Backhand Loop

The forehand loop can be played from most positions on the table, especially if you are fit and mobile. Backhand loops are less common. Some Hungarians, both men and women, became well-known for very good backhand loops, and now players from other countries are following in their footsteps.

You should not turn sideways for the backhand loop since it is a more square-on shot. As with the forehand, the bat can be taken below the knees and you should drive from the legs, as well as using your arm and waist. The backhand loop is harder than the forehand loop because it comes more from the arm and less from the body. You may, therefore, compensate by using more wrist. You can, however, get to a very high level indeed without making the shot part of your game. You can merely run round and hit a forehand loop from the backhand side instead.

Fig. 21c

Fig. 21d

Variety of loops

It is quite important to have a variety of loops. Try not to go on looping with the same speed and spin, but keep your opponent guessing. Try, too, to keep him guessing by the preparation you make for each shot. Don't advertise the fact that the same loop is on the way. You can sometimes mix a slow loop with a fast loop, or build up from slow loops to fast ones.

With a fast loop you are really driving the ball. Do not attempt this against a chopped ball, but against one that has been floated or blocked. To execute a fast loop, close the bat angle and move forwards. You will still get some spin but not as much as with a slow loop. So you can produce high and kicking loops (slow loops) or low and fast loops.

Sidespin Loops

You can also produce sidespin loops. These can only really be done on the forehand. As the bat goes around the outside of the

55

ball, the body tends to go round with it and sometimes the right leg follows it as well. You swivel on the left leg as the bat comes from behind your body, across, round and in front of you. This makes the ball pitch sideways after striking the table and it can be extremely effective when taking the ball very wide to the opponent's forehand.

Fig. 22, another photograph of the loop, shows the intensity of concentration that is needed in a match. The eyes are rivetted on the ball and you can tell from the facial expression that the mind is absolutely on the task. The picture also provides an example of how the forehand loop can be played quite effectively from the backhand side of the table.

If your opponent is looping you have to watch carefully for signs of what he or she is doing with the ball. With the very heavy looped topspin the opponent's bat angle will be more

Fig. 22 Forehand loop.

closed. You may have to adapt your reply with every single stroke because your opponent may do something different each time. A good example of this type of player is the German Kirsten Kruger who has often played with long pimples on one side of her bat and reversed pimples on the other side. One shot she hits with the reverse; the next she turns her bat round behind her back and plays exactly the same stroke but with the pimples, so creating a different spin. You must look closely at the flight of the ball to see how it is spinning, but even though you may be concentrating very hard you may still make mistakes. However, you will become accustomed to it after a while, and remember, a good player will always be able to counter the loop.

9 The Smash and the Lob

The smash is often a natural follow-up to a good loop. It should enable you to finish off a rally once you have your opponent at a disadvantage. If you cannot smash, it is a great comfort to an opponent, who may then risk lobbing the ball up in the knowledge that you are not likely to put the ball away. This can be tiring for you and an encouraging method of defence for him. A poor smasher may find an opponent escapes from all sorts of situations where the point had almost been lost.

A few players are so good with the smash that they are able to play it from many different positions and in a number of situations. They can even smash a low ball, so excellent is their timing. It is then a devastating shot to mix with the topspin attack. But most players, certainly to begin with, are better off waiting for the ball that comes above net height before they consider smashing.

Forehand Smash

To play this shot properly you must have your body weight moving to the right and forwards. You need to put as much force into the ball as possible, but at the same time it is important to get well over it otherwise it can easily disappear off the end of the table. The ball is struck flat to get as much power as possible so there is little or no spin to help ensure the ball goes on. A little movement of the wrist can be a good thing because it will help to give you extra force.

In the first photograph from the sequence of the forehand smash (fig. 23a), the bat is taken well back and the weight is on the right foot. Eyes are on the ball. This ball is a high one, but if

Fig. 23a Forehand smash sequence.

Fig. 23b

Fig. 23c

59

it had been lower and quicker the backswing would need to have been more restricted. As you can see from the second photograph (fig. 23b) the bat comes from below the ball and the weight has been transferred onto the left foot. The ball is about to be hit flat, and eyes are still firmly fixed on it.

In the third photograph (fig. 23c) the ball has been hit as hard as possible. The arm, moving from the shoulder, has supplied much of the power, but there has been a small snap of the wrist as well. Transferring the weight to help give power is important to most strokes, but never more so than to this one. In this particular shot it has caused the trunk to turn from a half-sideways position (fig. 23a) through about a ninety-degrees turn (fig. 23c). The follow-through whips past the head. Although there is plenty of commitment about the shot, there is no question of finishing off balance. As you can see from fig. 23c it is possible to get back to a ready position—in a game your opponent might block the ball back (see Chapter 10) and you might have to be prepared to play another smash.

Occasionally, it is necessary to commit yourself. You might, for instance, find you want to come round the side of the table. A backhand smash is hard to do and so is rarely seen; it is sometimes better to move round and hit the ball with your forehand if the ball is high enough. You can hit harder and very often more accurately with the forehand. And from the backhand side of the table you can often get a good angle to put the ball away.

Fig. 24 shows the smash from the side of the table. The picture also gives an impression of the rhythm of the shot (as always both timing and rhythm are essential). There is a lot of body movement in a forward direction, especially from the waist and trunk. The bat finished in a closed, almost horizontal, position. This was not because there is topspin on the shot—remember it is hit flat—but because it is natural and comfortable to do so. The feet are also clearly shown, way out beyond the side of the table, and the weight is mainly on the left foot.

The ball has been struck from behind the baseline in the picture but it will, of course, be much easier to smash a half-table ball. In such circumstances you would be able to smash quite a low ball. Conversely, if the ball were to land to a good length right on the baseline, it might need to come up quite a long way before you could smash it.

When the ball bounces up high your preparation might be

Fig. 24 The forehand smash seen from the side of the table.

different from that shown in photographs *a-c* in which it starts from below the ball. You may decide to take the bat above the ball instead, and bring it sharply down, although you will need to make sure you get well to the side of it. This can sometimes be more difficult with a lobbed ball, especially if there is topspin on it; then it may come up quite high and be hard to control. To ensure getting over the ball, some players jump off the ground and smash with their body weight coming down. If the defender does lob the ball deep near the baseline, there is a very reasonable chance of still being able to win the rally. By forcing the attacker to smash from great heights and distances it can be possible to take advantage of the fact that a light celluloid ball slows down considerably. The defender can go on retrieving it for a long time while the attacker is having to deal with a ball that is less easy to control than it appears. Such lobbing and smashing rallies, which spectators love, often end with the attacker making a mistake.

Apart from playing the role of hero in these spectacular rallies, there can be other good reasons why a defender should want to risk getting involved in them. They can be tiring for the attacker and may sap his strength. Also, just one miss with a smash from a lob can lower a player's morale, if only momentarily.

For these reasons a defender may win points in the rallies that follow, even though they may be played in a different way. This is why Jacques Secretin of France, a former European champion, sometimes risks losing a couple of points by lobbing early in the match. He likes to see what the effect is. Only the better players should risk this, but the lob can still be a useful shot in anybody's armoury.

The Lob

The lob only becomes really effective if it is hit high and with topspin. Then it enables a player to recover into a reasonable position and also makes the ball leap upwards and forwards

Fig. 25 The lob.

when it strikes the table. All this means the ball has to be hit quite hard. The follow-through is above the head as in fig. 25.

The first lob in a rally is likely to be played by the defender when he or she has been caught out of position. Once you are a long way from the table and wide, as in the photograph, it is hard to chop the ball accurately all the way back to the table. You are more likely to be concentrating on getting the ball back the best way you can. If you do this by sending the ball high, you have a better chance of recovering into an improved position next time. Then, with a little more time to play the shot, you may be able to put topspin on the ball. Generally, you will have to go on lobbing until the point has been won or lost. Occasionally, the opponent may give up the attack or the defender will be in a position to do a counter-attacking topspin.

Remember, to create topspin you need to take the bat down low and hit up the back of the ball with a brushing action. The ball then rotates forwards. You should be careful not to hit the ball level with your face as this would be too high and would make topspinning difficult. Let the ball drop and try to play a natural topspin stroke even if you are under pressure. Push with your legs to get extra topspin. The shot will obviously be more easy on the forehand where you can get more spin. On the backhand lob you should hit the ball facing square on.

The lob is often an enjoyable shot. It is a nice feeling when an opponent is trying to put the ball away while you frustrate every attempt in a spectacular fashion. Most spectators want the defender scrambling around at the back to win the rally, and in fact the lobber often looks to be in a worse position than he or she really is. It is necessary, of course, to be a good mover and you will need to train properly (see Chapter 12).

10 The Block

The blocking type of game is not to be encouraged for beginners: you need excellent reflexes and a very good touch. But it has become an important part of the modern game because, if done well, the block can enable a player to win back the initiative immediately. There are a few players who have developed a special ability for blocking, and some have even based a close-to-the-table style on it, such as Desmond Douglas and Wilfried Lieck of West Germany. For other players it is a useful shot when caught in a difficult situation. It is not, however, something that can easily be taught. Blocking will probably just come naturally to you.

Backhand Block

In fig. 26 of the backhand block the shot does not look particularly difficult, but really it requires a lot of control. Done properly, it is like providing a cushion for the ball. You cannot block a chop but only a fast ball, cushioning it against the speed and the spin. In taking the speed and the spin out of the opponent's hit, loop or topspin drive, you can send it back low or short, or both.

Blocks can be produced in different ways. Desmond Douglas sometimes makes a more powerful block by hitting through it without cushioning the ball at all. Then he is able to force the ball all around the table. But usually the block is used to control the opponent's topspin. The bat is placed at a closed angle over the ball to keep it down. You can see in the photograph that the bat is tilted over the ball. How much it is tilted depends on how

Fig. 26 The backhand block.

much topspin has been produced. Obviously you have to get further over the ball if your opponent has put a lot of spin on it.

This is not always as easy to do as it seems. In fig. 27 (see over) Desmond Douglas has contained an opponent's attack with his famous backhand block. He has received his opponent's speed and spin at full blast and has had to leap off the ground to keep the ball down. This is not ideal, and not to be recommended, but the picture does show the tremendous speed, as well as the compensation of the bat and the body weight, that is sometimes necessary.

At times it is best to block flat. Sometimes you need to close the bat over the ball a fraction, and occasionally you can even put a little bit of chop on a block. You will find your own best way.

Fig. 27

Block against a flat forehand

The block can be made against a flat forehand hit without too much difficulty and that is the best way to start learning the stroke. You simply place your bat and learn to control the ball by developing the feeling in your fingers and in your hand. It will be harder when you try to control a topspin ball.

Forehand Block

Much is the same for the forehand block (see fig. 28) as for the backhand block. Once again the angle of the bat depends on how much spin is on the ball. The bat will be closed for a heavy topspin and opened out for a shot with less spin. It is slightly closed in this picture, although not quite so much as in the picture of the backhand block where the ball is being touched down over the net. Both blocks have been played against loops but you can sometimes block against a smash as well. If you do, the bat angle will need to be more vertical, and then it requires excellent reflexes. If you can execute a forehand block the ball may go for a winner as your opponent receives a lightning return from his own speedy attack.

Blocking the ball short

Sometimes you can block the ball very short, and if you can so manage it that the second bounce would also land on the table if allowed to, you should prevent the opponent from getting in

Fig. 28 The forehand block.

with another loop. Desmond Douglas has been an expert at this, especially against the top Hungarians who produce heavy topspins away from the table. Desmond varies his blocks, blocking soft by taking the bat back slightly on impact, and this makes the opponent move in. If the opponent then attacks, Desmond blocks the next one hard, forcing him out again.

The block has become more frequently used in recent times, because with more players around favouring the loop the most likely responses are to block or to chop. Unfortunately, there are not as many players using the chop as there should be. Looping against a loop is another possible response, but it is more difficult.

Points to note

As you can see from the three photographs you do not need to turn sideways for the block. You can face straight down the table—indeed, often there is no time to do anything else. But you cannot simply stand upright: you have to use your body. The body has to be in sympathy with the shot and slightly bent over the ball, because the connection between the body and the arm is important in helping to guide the ball.

There is a tendency to reach for a wide ball rather than to get your feet there first. If the ball is unexpected or very fast you may not have a choice. But it is better to get into the right position, even for a difficult, speedy block. Practise by making yourself move your feet immediately as well as your arm. Then you will not tend to lean over, off balance. At the same time the block is the one shot, more than any other, where you have to improvise. Reactions and feeling for the ball are all-important.

11 Materials

The materials that are put on the bat—the rubber and the sponge—can add a whole new dimension to a player's game. As mentioned earlier, there are many different combinations of materials that are used in the modern game. One combination about which there has been controversy in the past is the use of long pimples on one side of the bat and reversed rubber on the other.

When the Chinese first brought out this combination opponents did not know what to expect and so made a lot of mistakes. The bats produced such a variety of unexpected spins that many points were won straight from serve. Long pimples were also particularly effective in counteracting a hard drive or any heavy spin. Some players got used to the long pimples and now they have become more or less accepted everywhere. They can be countered, but clever use of this combination, or indeed of other combinations, can still be effective.

Types of Combination Bats

The most usual combinations are reverse rubber with:
  (a) long pimples
  (b) long pimples plus sponge
  (c) anti-loop rubber
  (d) normal pimples plus sponge.

Short pimples produce a different speed and propel the ball slower with less spin. The length and flexibility of the long pimples are very important—it is no good if they are not flexible because they will not have much effect. At best they provide a puzzling variety of effects: serving sometimes produces no spin, defending often provides a great deal of different spins.

Advantages to be gained by use of combination bats
Twiddling
If you do use a combination bat, you should learn how to use the combination properly. The greatest advantage is often obtained by twiddling the bat to use both surfaces for backhand and forehand. This is difficult because it may mean you have to use twice as many strokes as the normal player does. There will be a different bat angle and a different follow-through for the same stroke with a different rubber. There are players, usually the attacking combination-bat players, who stick to one surface for one wing. Either way you will need to have mastered the basics of the game before you try.

With backhand chop and float
Using the long pimples on the backhand chop and float services produces a ball that has no spin. The reverse rubber produces a very heavy chop. One of the best ways to tell the difference is from the angle of the bat, but some players, notably Desmond Douglas, listen to the sound. There will also be a slight difference in the flight. The ball comes over the table faster with the reverse rubber.

Backhand serve
Most of the time on the backhand serve you float the ball (no spin) with the pimples and chop with the reverse. You cannot play a chop serve with the pimples but you can float the ball with the reverse. With the sidespin chop serve, crouching down, you can use both sides. The opponent expects the spin which the reverse provides, but if you use the pimples with the same kind of action then there is very little spin. The opponent tries to counter a sidespin chop when it is actually a float, and a mistake is likely to be made.

There are many ways to deceive the receiver. The opponent can be encouraged to think the serve is going to be a backhand chop, then at the last moment the ball can be put wide to the backhand and served fast, with a topspin action; the opponent would expect a low serve.

During the rallies, too, there can be many opportunities to turn the bat and fool the opponent. If you are using the long pimples on the push it will not create much spin, and the reverse is the side you will need to use to put backspin on the ball. It is the mixture of spin and no spin that can be particularly deceiving.

Defensive strokes
With the truly defensive strokes, like chopping and floating, the long pimples come into their own. Spin from long pimples comes mostly from what the opponent has already put on the ball. A heavy topspin will be chopped back with a very heavy backspin.

Sometimes long pimples are also used in attack, but usually then the player will not twiddle. The pimples can, for instance, be used by a player close to the table to block on the backhand, drawing the opponent in, while the forehand is used for powerful attack, pushing the opponent back.

It can be a pleasurable feeling knowing what spin you are about to put on the ball and that the opponent does not know. It can be very difficult to summon up the concentration needed to play against combination bats.

Remember, though, that since 1983 it is illegal to stamp while playing a shot (players used to do this to hide the sounds of the different rubbers). It also became illegal to twiddle the bat under the table on service or to hide the bat with your body—two other previously popular ploys used by combination bat players. And since 1984 different colours on each side became necessary. Remember, too, you need to have mastered everything already described in this book before you should begin to consider using one of these bats.

12 Tactics, Fitness, Psychology

Tactics can win matches. If you are an all-round player, you will have more tactical choices and therefore more ways of winning matches. But even if you are primarily a defensive or attacking player, there are tactical varieties you can use that will make a big difference to your results.

Avoid playing the ball to a medium length. Close to the net, or at the base of the table—those are the places to aim at. Never play 'half table', as it is sometimes called. Also note your opponent's weaknesses and make sure you take advantage of them. Some players keep a note of opponents' characteristics, such as where they tend to put the ball or what kind of serves they use. Learn to notice as many things as possible and act on them. Even a talented opponent is only as good as his weakness if this is exposed.

If you can expose a weakness, train yourself to observe the effect it has on your opponent. Sometimes a weakness can gradually become stronger, or even a strength, if pressured for too long, and that can even occur during the course of a single match. If so, variety will become the key. Variety can sometimes be used to break down the apparently strong aspects of an opponent's game.

Defender's Tactics

A defender wins principally by being accurate and by disguising spin. You rely on keeping the ball in play and forcing the attacker into a mistake. The defender, therefore, needs not so much variety of shot, but variety of speed, placement and degree of spin. Slight variations each time can be crucial, preventing the attacker from taking liberties or luring him to overstretch his ability.

Attacker's Tactics

The attacker's tactics depend more on the kind of opponent he has—a 'blocker', a 'chopper', or a player similar to himself. He might need to use different degrees of topspin and pace to upset a blocker's timing. But against a rival looper he may need to get in first as often as possible. Against a defender he may wait, perhaps playing the ball short before attacking, and then playing it short and long to bring the defender in and out.

It is useful to notice whether a 'looper' plays better close to the table or away from it. Is he more effective when given a ball to the wings (either side of the table)? If so, play further to the middle. He may well become flustered with a ball hit straight at him if he stands close to the table. Some players sense these tactics by instinct; others need to learn how to work it all out.

Planning Tactics
Playing against the same opponent twice does not mean that he is going to perform the same way as last time. No good going on with a tactic if things are not working according to plan that day. Be ready to try something different. Ideas are good servants but bad masters.

Opponents may play differently at different times of the same match as well. Some players may be more afraid to take risks when the score is close towards the end of a game. A few may be more likely to take a chance. Nearly all players will react slightly differently in a crisis situation. At such moments you may find that you are successful by providing the unexpected.

Fitness

There was a time when table tennis was not regarded as very physical. Some still think of it as a game in which players stand by a table tapping the ball short distances. A look at modern table tennis will show how wrong this is.

There is a great deal of movement, a vast number of strokes requiring fine footwork and balance, and looping, lobbing and smashing rallies that are often quite spectacular. Even at a middle-range level, players wind themselves up to play a loop and the ball may be hit at distances of up to forty feet if both players are away from the table. Watch a good defender and you will see how much hard work has to be done if he is to chop and float consistently.

We have made frequent references to the need to move the feet quickly and to have the weight in the right position. There is a tendency, when a ball is moving fast and wide, to reach first and move afterwards. Getting into the habit of moving the feet immediately is very important. Quick recovery between each shot is crucial, so it pays to be light on your feet.

There are many kinds of fitness and it is not possible to lay down hard and fast rules as to how you should work to achieve it. Each person's physical characteristics will be different. And different kinds of training can be developed depending on the type of player.

Endurance, power, speed, and suppleness are all different qualities of fitness, and all valuable to work on. Power is necessary for the all-out attacker and the large discus action movements of the topspin shots. Speed of hand, foot and eye are vital to the 'close-to-the-table' player for blocking and counter-hitting. Suppleness and endurance are necessary for any good player. Table tennis demands a whole variety of movements and it is important that your body is free to change direction comfortably. In a tournament you may have to play several times a day, so it is no good if you cannot keep going.

Weight training and circuit training are useful to build up strength for the power player, sprinting can be good for the speed player, and running and jogging good for endurance. Warming-up exercises with the neck, arms, trunk and legs are useful preparation for both playing and training. There is also shadow play, which reproduces the movements made in a match.

Regular practice will also help get you fit. It is possible to develop a way of playing that operates deliberately within your physical limitations. If you can do this you should try to stretch those limitations. Don't practise simply by playing. Practise each shot in turn, meticulously, preferably getting someone better than yourself to feed the ball to you. If you have someone who is good at feeding, begin by staying in one place and trying to groove the arm and wrist movements. When this has been done, turn and move the body into the shot to build up rhythm. Finally, move the feet into the shot and back into the ready position.

Psychological Fitness

Getting physically fitter will make you psychologically stronger. You will feel more confident. Preparing for matches with adequate training and practice not only helps you become more skilful but it also helps concentration and determination. However, you may need to do more than this to become psychologically prepared to play in a match.

In many matches there is little to choose between the skill of the players, nor may there be much to choose between them in their physical preparation. If so, the difference between a winner and a loser may be decided by who is fitter in mind.

The power of the mind to influence performance is tremendous and is greatly underestimated. There have been countless instances where technically inferior players have won matches because of the strength of their attitude. There are many things you can do to get the best from yourself.

The first is that of learning to think positively, to have a good attitude. This means keeping in mind reasons why it is possible to win, rather than dwelling too much on problems and obstacles. And it can be worth spending time before each match emptying your mind of any problems unrelated to the games in hand. Build your resolve to do your best. Think of not only why you can do well, but how.

It sounds simple but it isn't. One way to short-cut a lot of difficulties is to know yourself. Try to become aware of what you are feeling before you play and—not so easy—while you play. You will then stand a better chance of adopting the best preparation for you personally.

Some international players have practised mental preparation by calisthenics. This is a form of meditation. It involves trying to empty your mind and then thinking 'warm', thinking 'heavy'. It aids relaxation, but it does not by any means suit everybody. Some players have very different ways of preparing and only they know how to do it. Some like to go away quietly on their own; some like to talk to people to keep calm. Spend a little time working out what suits you.

One thing you should have in common with all players is feeling nervous before a match. Without this, and the build-up of adrenalin that enhances mental attitude and physical faculties, you will not be able to do your very best. Don't worry too much about being nervous, simply be concerned to keep it within reasonable bounds. Nervousness will only hinder you if it is really excessive.

A good way of coping with it is to think of the tactics you plan to adopt. Think too of the conditions you are expecting to encounter (lighting, speed of table, etc.), of your strengths and the opponent's weaknesses, and of your physical warm-ups. These all help to use nervous energy. Talk things over with coach, colleagues, family or friends, if it helps. If you need peace and quiet, make sure you get it.

When you actually start to play try to keep your mind flexible. Are conditions fast or slow, is the opponent doing roughly what you expected and are you adapting? But above all, don't neglect matters of the mind. They have a powerful influence.

13 Postscript

The popularity of table tennis has grown steadily during the twentieth century and there is every indication that this popularity will continue. Prices have risen and will probably continue to do so, but table tennis is likely to stay a relatively cheap game to play.

More and more players at lower levels of the game go about enjoying their sport in a more organised, purposeful way. Although thousands play the game for fun in their homes, an increased number regard it as a competitive sport. They dress properly for it, they practise, they compete. They treat their games with a degree of seriousness—and almost certainly get more enjoyment from it as a result.

At higher levels more players are playing full-time, and a few manage to make a living from it. Prize money is improving even for the part-time player, and professionalism is taking its first tentative steps. The development of table tennis as a spectator sport, with more sponsorship and more television coverage, is likely to take time, but playing standards are rapidly rising and rubber technology is becoming ever more sophisticated, thus improving the standard of equipment.

All these improvements and new developments can easily be spoilt if the people involved in table tennis change in the wrong way. Other developing sports have sometimes been blighted by greed, cynicism and bad behaviour. Table tennis has had a reputation for decency and sportsmanship, and for creating happiness among many people. To the players of the future this reputation is entrusted.

14 Glossary

Anti-loop Rubber that has a deadening effect upon the ball, thus destroying the spin from a chop or a loop.

Backhand Shot played on the opposite side of the body from the playing arm.

Backspin Ball made to spin round in the air towards the hitter as the ball travels towards the opponent.

Baseline Popular term for the official name of the endline: the white line on the edge of the end of the table.

Block A shot that is played close to the table with little movement of the bat, transforming defence into attack.

Chop A defensive shot that produces backspin.

Combination bat Bat with different playing surfaces on each side.

Drop shot A very short shot that drops near enough to the net to bounce several times on the table.

Float A defensive shot that looks like a chop but produces little or no spin.

Forehand Shot played on the same side of the body as the playing arm.

Lob A defensive shot that goes very high in the air.

Loop Shot played with such heavy topspin that the ball moves through the air in a large loop, upwards and then downwards before landing on the table.

Push A basic, controlled shot with limited backswing and follow-through.

Rubber Playing surface glued on to the bat.

Sandwich bat Bat that contains, in order, wood, sponge, and rubber in layers (looks like a sandwich from the side).

Sidelines White lines on the edges of either side of the table.

Sidespin Ball made to spin round in the air to either side of the table as it travels towards the opponent.

Smash A hard, flat attempt at a winner. If successful it is called a kill.

Topspin Ball made to spin round in the air towards the opponent as it travels towards the opponent.

15 Useful Addresses

The English Table Tennis Association,
21 Claremont, Hastings, East Sussex.
Telephone: (0424) 433121

The International Table Tennis Federation,
53 London Road, St Leonards-on-Sea, East Sussex.
Telephone: (0424) 430971

16 Index